I0415010

Blood in and Blood out

By:Anthony Hawkins

ISBN:978-1-300-54626-9

Dedicated to the gay and lesbian community

Prologue

John was one of the brightest students in his class,he was also known as the most quiet one on campus.He was in his second year of college,he was the average guy,but he held a dark secret.He didn't have many relatives,the ones he did have were sick or dead.His mother was on life support,battling against cancer.And his father was dead,an unfortunate fate,caused by his drug dealing lifestyle.

John didn't want to follow in his fathers footsteps,but he believed he had no choice,either watch his mother die,and drop out of college or keep hustling.That way he could afford to pay for cancer treatments and school.John rushed home from school,knowing he had a tight shift that day.

Chapter 1

It took you hours to get here man,you know Tyrelle dont play that shit! A voice spoke.Look man! I have school and a whole lot of other shit on my plate,so dont bug me with that shit right now,John said,his face fuming with anger.

Listen lil homie! you gonna get a cap busted in your ass,if you keep fucking with Tyrelle's money.Is Tyrelle peddling this shit or me? John questioned.You are a brave ass lil nigga,i gotta give it to you,the man said,meeting John's gaze.I dont like being brave,im only brave because i have to be,John said,a small tear rolling down his cheek.

You know,for you to be as fearless as you are,you sensitive as hell,the man chuckled.I got you,i'll tell Tyrelle that it was my fault,i'll take the heat this time.This time only dude.

Thank's Scoop,John said,brushing the tears from his eyes and coat.Take this shit,Scoop said,tucking a small jet black pistol into John's coat.

John flinched,he saw guns,but he never held one,he always had protection nearby.Jeffrey got jacked the other day,they stole everything he had on him,so you might need that.So,where he at now,he alright? John awaited Scoop's reply.

Hell naw he ain't alright,they put three bullets in him,after robbing him.And the same dudes who got him was found dead,i dont understand how you get multiple stab wounds when you packing heat like them? Scoop's face became puzzled.That is some weird shit,John replied.Stay safe dude,Scoop said,handing John five packs of their stock.

John went to work,selling three bags in less than an hour.The abandoned warehouse was the easiest place to sale.That was the hot spot,everyone sold or brought there.But getting big spenders there was the problem,the bigger fish only came there on certain occasions.

John mostly worked the streets,but sold the other two bags at the warehouse,knowing that it would be big game there,that day.

John was done,the sun began to set.

Chapter 2

The big spenders only came during late hours or latenight.John headed back to Tyrelle's place,still counting the profit he made from his drug sales.Tyrelle's door was open,this was out of the ordinary,especially for Tyrelle.

John entered,his nerves pushing to the surface.Come in man! It's cool,a deep voice said.John shut the door,as he entered.The house was completely dark,and empty.There was only one light on,the one in the kitchen.

John walked towards the kitchen,spotting patterns of blood,on the hardwood floor.He paused.Move your ass nigga,the voice said again.It was Tyrelle,he sat at the table,his gun tilted from his hand.

Tyrelle tapped his gun against the marble frame.Sit down! Tyrelle said,his eyes locked on John.

It's blood all over the floor,John said as he sat in the chair.Yea,i know,Tyrelle said smoothly.It's from this nigga right here,Tyrelle said,pulling a bloodied and lifeless Scoop to the edge of the table.What happened? John said,already knowing the answer.

He was late,that's what happened.Tyrelle stood from the table.John jumped to his feet,not knowing what was about to happen.Tyrelle pushed his body into John's,before John could make a move,pinning him to the wall.

I got your money,here,John reached into his pockets,pushing the money to Tyrelle's waist.You trying touch my dick,you a faggot ass nigga,Tyrelle said as his nose flared.Im trying give you your money,that's all.We going play a game,since you like touching nigga's dicks.

Tyrelle pulled John's hand toward his crotch,while pushing his gun into John's temple.John's hand started to shake,fear swelling inside him.The moment your hand reach the tip of my dick,your ass is six feet under,Tyrelle whispered into John's ear,still guiding John's hand down his pelvis.John flinched,something hard tugged against his coat pocket.John pulled the black pistol from his coat,pressing it into Tyrelle's chest.Tyrelle paused.He was shocked,but not impressed.

So,you going shoot me,You aint got the heart,Tyrelle said with a smirk.I will,just back the fuck up,John said,his body tense.

No,you aint,you know why? It's because your ass got feelings for me,Tyrelle said,in a whisper,his face becoming blank.I was the only one who gave you money to get on your feet,after your pops died.You secretly look at me as your mentor,be truthful.John froze.Tyrelle grabbed the gun from John's hand,placing both guns to John's neck.

I should kill you,Tyrelle said,his chin to John's left cheek.Any other person i would do,right here and now,but im not even going to waist my bullets,Tyrelle spoke,his lips pressing into John's cheek.John could feel Tyrelle's breath pouring down his neck.

Tyrelle moved his lips towards John's,their lips almost made impact.Tyrelle started to breath deeper.I bet you like me being all over you like this,dont chu? You always been the sensitive type,Tyrelle said,in a deep voice.

He slid his lips across John's,then pushed his tongue into John's mouth,french kissing him.Three tears fell from John's eyes.Tyrelle released his lips from

John's,then headed to the door,pushing the guns in his pockets.

Take care of that,Tyrelle said,pointing to Scoop's dead body.That shit better be gone,once i get back.And dont get any ideas dude,i was just trying to break your motherfucking spirit.Tyrelle shut the door,on his way out.John remain still and silent,his body shivering.He had work to do,and quick.

John finally came to his senses.He began mopping the floor,he then searched the whole house,trying to find something big enough to put the body in.

He paced and paced up and down the living room.A thought flickered in his head.He pushed every piece of furniture to the left side of the room,pulling and jerking the big carpet,from under the furniture.

He used the little strength he had to drag Scoop's dead body into the center of the rug.He began folding it,until the rug covered Scoop's entire body.The carpet began to fall out of place.

John rushed to the kitchen,grabbing a huge roll of duck tape,he began taping the carpet together.The tape held the carpet together,concealing Scoop's body inside.John dragged the body into his small nissan sentra.

He headed down to the nearest creek,dumping the body into the water.The water pulled the body back and forth,until sinking to the bottom.John started to breath heavily,this wasn't something he was used to.

The drugs was one thing,but the dead body was another.

John raced home,glancing over into his rear view mirror,unsure if anyone had seen him.It was dark out,but he was still paranoid.

The streets was clear,not a soul in sight,only a black cat,John saw running into the alley.John locked his car door,his hands shaking in the process.He headed back into the house.Tyrelle sat on the couch,his eyes following John as he came in.

John could smell a slight fragrance.It was perfume.Nigga you threw away my motherfucking carpet?! Tyrelle said.I had no where else to put the body,John explained.So,you really took it upon yourself to put that dead motherfucker in my shit?

You are a funny ass motherfucker,Tyrelle grinned.So,where you put the fucking body at? I dumped it in the creek,John murmured.I told you to get rid of the shit,not put the shit in the creek,dont you know that shit could float back up.

Man! you are a dumb motherfucker,Tyrelle said,his voice becoming even more deeper.So,did anybody see you?

Naw! wasn't nobody there,and it was dark out,John explained,fear gleaming upon his face.I did what you told me to do,the body is gone.

Shh! Shh! Nigga it's some bitches in the other room,Tyrelle said as two women entered the living room,from the bathroom.Did ya'll like that shit,ya'll better not had smoked that shit up,Tyrelle smiled at the women.

Hi! How you doing? one of the women said,her long braids covering her left eye.Im cool,John said,still standing silently.The other girl rolled her eyes,not saying a word.

The women sat on the couch with Tyrelle,one on each side.

That's Johnathan's lil dude Shannon! You aint going speak? Tyrelle said,staring at the woman,and then back to John.Didn't he die,i knew he favored somebody,but he was just sitting there? Aint the nigga's supposed to say hi first? Shannon said,with a slight frown.

He did motherfucking speak! Tyrelle said,his face becoming annoyed.I aint hear him,he got one of them low voices,like he gotta twitch or something.

Tyrelle yanked Shannon by her collar,her face became blank as Tyrelle held her in his grip.Bitch! You better show some motherfucking respect,i blast bitches too.

That lil dude picked up thirty kilos for me in one day.I should make you suck his motherfucking dick,Tyrelle said to Shannon,anger brushing across his face.

My bad,i was just joking with him,Shannon said,her nerves rushing to the surface.His pops showed me the game,now im going show him,Tyrelle said in a slight whisper.This is going be one bad ass lil nigga,once i get done with him.Tyrelle unzipped his pants,and then placed Shannon's head in his lap.

She could no longer talk.Tyrelle grabbed her hair as her head throbbed back and forth.Her hair concealed the full view of what was happening.Nigga your feet aint hurting,sit your ass down John,Tyrelle said in a moan.Tyrelle ripped Shannon's jacket off,while she continued.Here! Lay on that,get your ass some sleep,Tyrelle spoke,throwing Shannon's jacket to John.

John was tired,but became preoccupied with the deep slurping sounds escaping from Tyrelle's lap.The other woman cut off the lights.John kept one eye open,still watching.

I know you aint sleep nigga! Tyrelle said,barely catching his breath.You like that shit,dont you,Tyrelle chuckled.He stared directly into John's eyes,pushing Shannon's head down harder and faster.John still had nerves rushing in and out of him,but got a slight tingle in his loins.

He and Tyrelle made eye contact that entire night,until he drifted asleep.

Chapter 3

The hours passed,it was soon morning.John opened his eyes,the sun stung his eyes as he turned his head from the rays.

He turned back to the window,letting his eyes adjust to the sun.He was the only one there,Tyrelle and the women were no longer on the couch,but he was.

Someone had placed him on the couch.

John stood up,heading into the kitchen,the phone rang.Hello! John answered in his weary voice.Nigga you just now waking up? Tyrelle said.Yea,i am.

I left some money on the kitchen table.Go and get some shit for the house,and bring my motherfucking change back nigga,Tyrelle said.Nigga you got that?! Tyrelle spoke.Yea,im about to roll out now,John answered.

Alright! All good then,im downtown handling some business,and you hold it down,while im gone,Tyrelle said,before hanging up the phone.

John went to the corner store down the street.He ran a couple of errands,while he was out.He came back,unpacking everything he had brought from the store.It only took him ten minutes to finish.

He headed upstairs,after he was done.He hopped in the shower,letting the hot water run down his face and body,thinking about his life,good memories and the bad ones.

John began to hear the bathroom door open,the screechy sound hit his ears.It was Tyrelle.John pulled the shower curtain,instinctively.Nigga i seen it all before,aint no need in playing shy motherfucker.

Tyrelle stood over the toilet,then unzipped his dark blue denim jeans.Ah! Damn that feels good,i had to piss like fuck,Tyrelle moaned.Why didn't you use the bathroom downstairs? John questioned Tyrelle.

Because i didn't want to,thats why,stop acting like a pussy,your moms used to give us baths together all the damn time,Tyrelle said,pulling his manhood back into his pants.

We was kids,i was seven,and you was nine,and we didn't have a choice,John said in a low tone.True that,but like it or not,we was bubble buddies motherfucker.And by the way,i visited your moms.

You visited who? John said nervously.Your moms! Stop tripping,she was like a mother to me too,Tyrelle said in a sincere tone.Nigga you know my mother wasn't shit,neither was my fucking father,Tyrelle said in a whisper.Your father might had did his dirt,but he did it for you and your moms,my father aint give a shit about nobody else,but his damn self,Tyrelle explained.

Me and you gotta stick together lil homie,we might not be torn from the same cloth,but we headed down the same path,Tyrelle said,he then became quiet.

He pulled the shower curtain back,his eyes locked on John's naked body.You got a lil bit of muscle on you now nigga,he grinned.John covered his genitals with his hands.

Tyrelle reached into the tub,punching John in the side,it was hard,but not enough to seriously damage him.Thats for being late with my shit,Tyrelle smirked.Im not on some gay shit,but I love you tho nigga,Tyrelle said,before leaving out the bathroom.

John feared Tyrelle,but in some way he trusted him.

John dried himself off,after finishing his shower.He headed into his room,pulling on a black shirt,a pair of blue jeans,and then placing on a pair of black and white nikes,finishing the look with a white nike hat.He dashed on a bit of cologne,afterwards.

Tyrelle entered the room,while John gathered a thick roll of cash,and his keys.Dude im glad you got all fresh and shit,because we gotta hit.This cat name

Frank gotta job for us,Tyrelle said,standing next to John.

Nigga pull your shit to the side,Tyrelle whispered,pulling John's cap sideways.John didn't argue with him,but listened.Tyrelle wore his hat the same way.He had changed his previous outfit,now he wore black denim jeans,with a black tank top,exposing his long muscular arms.

He wore jordan shoes,a size twelve.His black durag covered his head.Tyrelle was good looking,but had the face of a killer,someone you wouldn't want to piss off.His tattoo gleamed from his right arm,the only tattoo on his caramel skin,a little darker from the hot sun.

He stood taller than John,six foot two.John wasn't short himself,but he still slightly towered over John.

John had a rich milky brown complexion,skin almost as soft and smooth as a babies.

Skin that would make the prettiest woman frown.His eyes sparkled,like an innocent childs,but he still contained masculine features,and his body was no childs.

Tyrelle slung a golden chain around John's neck,a chain worth at least a couple of grand.Nigga you gotta be iced out,Tyrelle said,staring into John's eyes,if we dont,these niggas going think we aint bringing in profit.And dont think i didn't know your motherfucking ass was the one running late,nigga you think im stupid,i ended Scoop ass as a fucking warning,you lucky i known your ass for so long nigga.

He pulled John by his shirt,they were face to face.Dont disappoint me cuz,Tyrelle whispered,in a way that was threatening,but soothing.Tyrelle's nostrils flared,his face appeared slightly angered,but enchanted.He finally let John loose.

Tyrelle was resisting something,something he wanted to succumb to.John tapped the edge of Tyrelle's hard arm.we cool,John whispered.Yea! We cool,are you motherfucking cool? Tyrelle smirked.They both cackled as they headed downstairs,and out of the front door.

John headed to his car,but Tyrelle yanked his arm,before he could pull out his keys.Nigga we aint taking your wack ass ride,we taken mine,Tyrelle smirked.Tyrelle took off his alarm as they headed towards the expensive car.John opened the passenger door.

Nigga get your ass in the back,we picking up some big fish nigga.John closed the door,then got in the back seat,the seats felt like butter.They pulled off.Tyrelle speeded through the trees as they entered the highway,they were no longer in the ghetto inner city,but traveling to a different area.

They finally approached a big mansion like house.Be respectful dude,these cats aint no joke,Tyrelle whispered to John.Nigga you playing with the chain? Tyrelle questioned.Naw,it was just tickling my neck,John replied.Nigga you like a child,Tyrelle grinned.

It wasn't the chain,it was his nerves getting the best of him.They headed up the stairs,Tyrelle rang the door bell.A tall dark skinned man answered.His eyes locked on Tyrelle and John.We here to see Frank,Tyrelle said,awaiting the mans answer.

Whats your partie? The man answered.Third street nigga,Tyrelle said,becoming annoyed.The man flipped his coat open,calmly,revealing a pistol,tucked in his coat pocket.Tyrelle lifted the end of his left pants leg,exposing two guns,on each side of his leg,wrapped in a band.I got pieces too nigga,Tyrelle smirked.

Tyrelle's smirk appeared polite,but had a dangerous meaning behind it.

The man grunted,then turned.Frank! You have visitors.A man approached the door,his skin pale,his hair jet black.He was italian.He spoke with a slight accent.He smacked the man through the face,disciplining him,like a child.You should have known who this was,the man said with hand gestures.He looked to Tyrelle,and then to John.

His eyes focused on John's features.Fuck me! The man said with excitement.

The man grabbed John's arm,squeezing John tightly to his chest.You look just like your fucking father,go have a seat,make yourself at home,the man spoke.John headed towards the other side of the room.

He sat on a long leather sofa,He could see Tyrelle and Frank talking,but he couldn't hear them.Tyrelle approached the couch,sitting next to John.I cant believe it! Johnathan's little boy,in my crib,Frank chuckled.So,lets talk this through,Frank said,his face becoming serious.

I have two spots i want done,ill provide all the tools you'll need,i got snipers,lasers,and safe decoders.So,the two of you up for the job? Frank questioned.John's eyebrows twitched,he had no clue that they would be robbing someone.

John spoke,but his sentence was cut off,by Tyrelle.Yea! We up to it,Tyrelle said,slightly easing his eyes over at John.John became silent.Frank smiled,ok,my boy Joe will hook you up,and he'll be assisting you.Joe aint that motherfucker we met at the door,is he? Tyrelle asked.

Frank began to chuckle.Yea! But he's pretty reliable,and good with a gun,Frank laughed.Alright then,as long as that nigga dont cause trouble,Tyrelle said as he and John stood to their feet.

Another man entered the room,his eyes concentrated on Tyrelle and John.Their the fuckers who slowed our rountine down,The man said.Is that right? Frank questioned.Yea,im not going bullshit you,we came up kinda stiff this month,Tyrelle said,looking directly at Frank.

No! Im not talking about you Tyrelle,im talking about him,Frank whispered,turning his gaze to the other man.The man paused.Joe! Frank said,nodding his head towards the man.Joe pulled his gun from his coat,firing one shot at the mans head.

I dont tolerate snitches! Frank said as the mans lifeless body fell to the floor.

John's eyes widened,he was getting deeper and deeper into the lifestyle of crime and drugs.

Here! Take this,Frank said,dropping a stack of hundred dollar bills into John's pocket.It's a gift,Frank chuckled,you work for me,and you'll recieve even more.

Frank gave John a pat on the back,and then headed upstairs.He didn't give John the chance to thank him.Joe dragged the body into the next room.So! You pussies ready? Joe said,after dispatching the body.Pussy?! Nigga put your money where your mouth is,lets see who's the pussy,once we handle this gig,Tyrelle smirked.

It aint no thang,for me,but your homeboy seems like he's new school,Joe said,staring at John.Im going to tell you straight up,in this business,you gotta push or be pushed lil dude,Joe said,gazing at John.They all headed outside.

Joe brought a black bag with him,grabbing it on his way out.John sat in the back seat,while Tyrelle and Joe sat in the front,they began loading the guns,these weren't like the guns John was getting used to seeing,these one's were high tech,some had silencers,some had scope vision,and some even had lasers.

John flinched at the sight,knowing the damage they could cause.Joe snapped a fully loaded clip into one of the guns,then passed it back to John.The gun also had a laser.This is how you use the laser,Joe said,pulling John's hand to the different gadgets.

Nigga who you? His motherfucking teacher or something? Tyrelle said to Joe with annoyance.I'll teach him myself,you just sit back,and make sure your ass got your shit together,Tyrelle said,handing John a blade.

Thats incase of emergency,shit dont run out of bullets either,Tyrelle smirked.We just selling a couple of kilos right?! John stuttered.

The stuttering was caused by his fear.Hell naw! Joe laughed out.John knew where they were going,but pretended not to.He was nervous,holding onto his gun tightly as they pulled off.

They hit a couple of spots,before going to their target.Night began to fall.They pulled up to a dark abandoned house,the smell of marijuana exited from the house as a tall guy exited from the house.

The guy was light skinned,and had long cornrows,almost reaching his back.His jeans were baggy,and his pockets were full,full of ammo and drugs.This is Lala! Joe said,as the stranger entered the car.

John glanced over at the guy.It wasn't a guy at all.I know your ass aint get high,when you know what we about to do? Joe questioned.Naw! It was some bitches in there,they let me eat the skins,after i gave them hoes some weed,Lala grinned.

So do them bitches know you a female? Joe chuckled.Yea they do,they dont give a fuck,as long as they hitting that pipe,Lala responded.What's up with ya'll niggas? Lala said,bumping her fist to John's,and then Tyrelle's.You quiet! This your first time,aint it? She laughed,as she examined John's face.Yea,it is,John answered.Dont worry! I got your back,she giggled.

They pulled off,heading to the big spot.

Chapter 4

We here motherfuckers! Tyrelle said,turning to John,and then Joe,and then Lala.They had finally reached the big spot,this spot was the most important of all,their job had to be done.The house was big,almost as big as Frank's,but guarded by two men.Lala handle your shit,Joe said in a whisper.

John watched in fear,he didn't think women were weak,but he still saw Lala as being fragile.Lala stepped onto the stairs,as she headed toward the two men.Im here to buy,she whisperd at the guards.We have spots for that,one of the men said.

I know! Lala said,reaching into her back pocket,pulling a gun out.

She shot both men,before they could pull out their own weapons.The men dropped to the ground,they were dead.

John saw Lala's gun being fired as a flurry of fiery sparks,and then seeing smoke exit from the barrel,but could not hear the sound.Lala was using a silencer.John was shocked.

That's my bitch! Joe laughed.Im telling you,that broad is a beast.That bitch is a nigga trapped in a womans body cuz,Joe grinned,proud of Lala's work.

Nigga you know you about to kill a couple of motherfuckers while we here,Right?! Joe said,while glancing at John.These niggas aint completely innocent their damn selves,Joe laughed.

The nigga who owns this house was fucking Frank's wife.And now he fucking with Frank's profit,Joe whispered.They all headed to the door.Tyrelle eased John to the center of him and Joe,he seemed protective of John.

Joe shot the door knob off,kicking the door in.Lala entered first,she was tall,but fast.John was the last to enter.A man rushed from the stairs,about to fire,but

Joe locked his laser on the mans chest,taking him out instantly.

Four more armed men rushed to the staircase.The shootout began.Tyrelle took out two,while Joe finished off the other two,there was only one left,he dropped his gun.Nigga show us where your motherfucking head man in charge at,Tyrelle said,his voice deepened.

He's out,but i know where he keeps his stash,the man said,shaking with fear.Then show us where the motherfucking stash at nigga or become like your homeboys,Tyrelle said,pointing to the dead bodies laying on the staircase.

The man showed them the way.Tyrelle and Joe headed up the stairs first,followed by John and Lala.

The man led them to a room,the room appeared normal.The man squatted to the floor,removing the rug from the area.He slid the floorboard open,revealing a large safe.

Joe pushed the man out the way.He slid a small decoder across the safe,he soon unlocked the safe.Joe took handfuls of money,stuffing the money into a huge black bag.That nigga got anymore hot spots around here? Joe asked.Im not sure,the man answered nervously.

Lala snatched the man by his shirt,placing her gun to his head.Dude are you fucking lying to us? She questioned.Naw! Im serious,thats the only spot i know of,the man said,with a panicked voice.That nigga probably telling the truth,let's roll out ya'll,Joe grinned.Lala let the man escape her fingertips,with a smug grin.

They all headed to the door,but Joe turned back around,meeting the man with a smile.Nigga you served your purpose! Joe said,pointing his gun directly at the man.

John blocked the sound from his mind,to pretend he didn't hear the trigger being pulled,even after he saw the crimson blood paint the walls.Lala chuckled in the background.

Let's get out this camp,before 5 0 come,Tyrelle said,pulling John in front of him as they all headed downstairs.

John's heart began to race,this was real,and he was apart of it,he didn't spill any blood that night,but he could still smell the gun smoke,and see the images of blood and death course through his thoughts.

They hopped in the car,pulling off into the night.The tires scraped against the ground as they headed back on the road.

Ya'll know them niggas going be gunning for us,once they get back in town,Lala laughed.

I know,and that's why i got something for their asses,Joe chuckled,while pulling out a huge gun,not just any gun,but a new model.

Oh shit son! Lala chuckled.That shit got double barrels,a laser,and a motherfucking scope,she grinned.

That shit is sweet,Tyrelle said,while lighting a blunt,while still driving.Nigga get your ass up here,Tyrelle said to John,in a strained voice,releasing the smoke from his nostrils.

The woods blew by them,as they headed down the secluded highway.Joe stepped over the shift gear,squeezing inbetween John and Lala.

John crawled to the front seat,next to Tyrelle.

So,whats up dude? Was that some crazy shit,Tyrelle questioned John with a smirk,the blunt still hanging from his mouth.

Joe and Lala were in their own world,having a conversation amongst themselves.It was wild,i mean,im used to selling and shit,but not all this type of shit,John said in a whisper.

Get used to it nigga,Tyrelle smirked.Here! try this shit,it'll relax you.Tyrelle pulled the blunt from his lips,placing it inbetween John's fingertips.Take it in slow nigga,Tyrelle chuckled.

John hesitated.Nigga why you aint smoking it? You can suck niggas dicks,but you dont wanna smoke this shit,why,because it been in my mouth nigga?

John looked surprised,his pulse racing.Yea nigga! Dont look surprised now,i heard about you at boulevard station.Im cool,That's your motherfucking business,just keep it to yourself,and away from me nigga,Tyrelle grinned.

I aint suck nobody dick,i was just curious dude,John replied.Whatever nigga,all ya'll fags the same,Tyrelle chuckled.

John frowned,and then puffed the blunt,it didn't bother him at all.Damn nigga,is that your first time smoking that shit,Tyrelle said with disbelief.You know i laced that shit with something extra right,Tyrelle chuckled.

Yea,i know,that's why i checked it out,beforehand,not because your pussy eating ass lips was on it,John replied.

You a smart ass motherfucker,Tyrelle laughed out.It aint none of my business,but do you use protection with them niggas? Tyrelle asked John.Some of them faggot motherfuckers be having aids,Tyrelle said,with a serious face.

Naw! To be honest,i only kissed one dude,that was it,John replied.

What ya'll motherfuckers talking about? Joe said,entering the conversation.Nigga you gay? Joe questioned John.

Nigga i thought all ya'll motherfuckers pranced around like fairies in shit,Joe laughed,assuming that all gay men were feminine.

Nigga kill that shit,he fam,Lala said,joining in.

Im surprised Lala ass aint got aids,all them motherfucking clams she be eating,Joe laughed.

Nigga all gay people aint got aids,Lala laughed out.John pass that shit son,i wanna puff,Lala chuckled.

So! Nigga you really into that gay shit? I mean,i aint know a nigga like you could be gay,Damn,my ass is puzzled? Joe muttered.

Nigga what chu mean you aint know a nigga like him could be gay?! Lala chuckled,as she inhaled another puff.

My friend Jackie B is a tranny,that bitch just got out of jail for cutting a nigga up,nigga attacked her in the alley,when he found out she was a dude.He busted her lip,but she sliced that motherfucker like a fish.

His homeys be clowning his ass,but they aint going fuck with her,she run tricks and hits for Otto,Lala said,passing the blunt to Joe.

I know who you talking about now,Joe replied.You talking about manicure,they call that bitch manicure around my way,after that bitch dug this nigga face out,while he was trying to beat her ass.

Ay yo! Dont sleep on them motherfucking gays and trannies,Joe laughed.

The lezzies too motherfucker,Lala chuckled out,the blunt was getting to all of them.

Lezzies,lesbians,it's all the same,Joe chuckled,then placed the blunt in his mouth.

Smoke filled the car.

Everybody rolled their windows down,letting some of the smoke escape.John held onto his cap as the wind blew through the windows.

Everyone was high,but Tyrelle and John handled theirs the best.Nigga dont get us in a motherfucking accident,Lala laughed out,her eyes dazed and blood red.Joe was falling asleep.

Tyrelle gave John a smirk,then placed John's hand on the steering wheel,guiding John's hand.You aint never drove a car like this before nigga,have you? Tyrelle chuckled,staring into John's eyes.This shit is cool,but i seen better,John laughed,while steering along with Tyrelle.

You got jokes motherfucker,Tyrelle chuckled.Tyrelle pressed down on the gas as they speeded through the dark woods,through the open road.Tyrelle gave John another glance,his hands began to massage into John's.

John flinched,but kept his hands on the steering wheel.Their eyes connected for a split second.

Let me come back to your crib son,Lala chuckled,waiting for Tyrelle's reply.The ac aint working in that motherfucking house i be at,and them bitches probably got that place smelling like all tuna fish up in that bitch,Lala giggled.

Before we go anywhere,we need to get this paper to Frank,John whispered.

Oh shit! Im glad you said something nigga,i almost forgot,Joe laughed.At least he aint too fucked up,my ass is out of it,Lala chuckled.

My man on his a game,Tyrelle grinned,looking at John.

They took the money to Frank.Frank split the profit with all four of them.Did you put a bullet in that motherfuckers brain? Frank questioned Joe.Naw! That nigga wasn't even there,we capped half of his boys tho,Joe grinned.

Good work,Frank said with a smile.Next time im going to find out where and when this moterfuckers leaving town,and i need you to take him and whoevers with him out,by all means,Frank said in a sincere tone.

Roger thinks he's fucking invisible,but i see right through him,he fucked my wife,and now the motherfuckers going to pay with his fucking blood,Frank said in a deep voice.Frank wanted Roger dead,at any cost.

Frank rolled up five grand,gently placing it in John's pocket,and then smiled.I told you,you work for me,we all get paid,one happy fucking family,Frank chuckled.They all laughed.Thank's,John said,his face sincere.

Frank kissed John's hand,this isn't homo shit,this is just a custom in my family.

It shows respect,Frank smiled.John did the same.They both chuckled,until a bullet flew pass John and Frank's head,grazing John's cheek.

Chapter 5

The bullet hit the big glass framed picture on Frank's wall,shattering the glass,breaking the frame to pieces.Strap up!! Tyrelle yelled as everybody grabbed ahold of their guns.

Bullets flew through the windows,as John pushed Frank to the ground,before one of the bullets could hit Frank in the head.

Tyrelle and Joe ducked down,shooting at the dark figures approaching the house.Lala pulled out another gun,assisting Joe and Tyrelle.Frank's men headed downstairs,firing at the approaching force.

Three men busted through Frank's door,firing at Frank's men.They took one of Frank's men out.John grabbed Frank's hand,crawling behind a steel table.Another man came through Frank's back door,his face covered with a dark mask,his outfit laced with ammo,and weapons.

John barely knew Frank,but the man did make him feel welcome,and he knew John,since birth.The man approached Frank and John,but John shot him,in his left arm,instinctively,before he could fire at Frank.

The man moaned in pain,then pulled his gun back up,aiming at John this time.

Tyrelle shot the man five times,the man fell to the ground,his blood splashing on John and Frank.Lala and Joe continued firing,them and a couple of Frank's men.The shootout lasted for fifteen minutes,until sirens hit everyones ears.

Let's get the fuck outta here! The armed assassins spoke.They headed to their cars,doors slammed as they all pulled off,fleeing the sight.

You all get the fuck outta here,Frank whispered.Thank's,you are a fucking soldier,Frank chuckled,patting John's back,taking a minute to breath.

Tyrelle grabbed John's arm,pulling him with him as they ran to the car.

Joe and Lala jumped to the back seat,as Tyrelle and John jumped to the front seats.They all pulled off,the tires screeched as they drove away.

I told ya'll! I told ya'll! I just knew them niggas was going pull some shit like this,Lala said,catching her breath.Tyrelle headed into the woods,trying to ditch the cops,if they were following them.

I know a hotel,not too far from here,Joe explained,breathing heavily.Direct me then motherfucker! Tyrelle said,heading back onto the road.

Chapter 6

They headed to a hotel,the hotel was empty,only one newlywed couple in the suite.John paid the fee,for two nights,for four people.Tyrelle slapped another two hundred dollars on the desk,the bellboy smiled,showing them to their room.

Call me for anything,the man said,with his slight accent.Joe shut the door in the mans face,before he could speak again.The room was big,sectioned into two parts.The rooms were connected,but had a slide door,seperating them.Each room had two beds and a bathroom.

Lala and Joe shared a room,while John and Tyrelle shared one.Lala sat on the small sofa by the window.It's about to go down son,we all know Frank aint having that,he going call a squad of his dudes,Lala said,while still panting.

Them fools then fucked up now! Joe chuckled,putting his bag away.John went into the bathroom,checking his face,after being grazed by a bullet.His face was okay,just a slight mark.

Tyrelle took his guns from his pockets,placing them on the night stand.Nigga i need to relax,im all tense and shit,go get some cds from the car,Lala said,looking at Joe.

I'll be back,you got anything good Tyrelle? Joe qustioned.Yea! Check my glove compartment,dont be jacking none of my shit either nigga,Tyrelle said,sitting on the big bed.

It took only three minutes for Joe to get back,he headed back up the elevator,buzzing into the hotel room.

Pop this in,Joe said,handing Lala one of the cds he brought back.Lala pushed the play button on the player.There was nothing but rap songs on the disc.That's how they liked it.

Lala bounced her head,while Joe did the same.The hours flew pass.Lala was the first one to fall asleep,then joe.You alright man?! Tyrelle questioned as he studied John's face.

Take your shit off,Tyrelle said in a whisper.For what? John replied.Im trying make sure your ass aint got no bullet wounds,thats why.Tyrelle searched John's body as John took off his shirt and pants.

He kept his boxers and Tank top on.You cool,Tyrelle said.Go wash that motherfucking blood off your arms tho.Blood? John questioned.Yea! From that dude i popped,Tyrelle answered.

Tyrelle stood there.John waited for Tyrelle to leave.Aint nobody looking at you nigga,Tyrelle whispered.John slipped out of his underwear and undershirt,standing fully nude.

Tyrelle studied John for a second,and then headed to the bed.John let the water and soap run down his body,rinsing away the blood,and the tension he felt.

John felt another warm body enter the shower,it was Tyrelle.Nigga stop hogging the water,Tyrelle smirked.Dude?! What are you doing in here? John said nervously.

Nigga we both need to shower,and we need to head out early tomorrow morning,to check in with Frank.I should be worried about you looking at my dangeling nigga,Tyrelle chuckled.John got out,after twenty minutes,and then Tyrelle.

They aint got no towels in this motherfucker? Tyrelle said with annoyance.They in the closet,Joe said,handing John a towel.He had finished with a shower himself,as he stood in John and Tyrelle's doorway,with nothing but a towel around his waist,his muscular chest exposed.

Thank's,John said,not wanting to stare too long,he was attracted to men,but these weren't the right men to be attracted to.John wrapped the towel around his waist,then headed to his bed.

Tyrelle snatched one of the towels from Joe's hand,then headed beside John,drying himself off,then draping the towel around his waist.Joe came into their room,his eyes locked on John.

Nigga you just walking into our shit like you own it,Tyrelle said,his face fustrated.Joe brought the cd player into John and Tyrelle's room.

The music still played.A biggie smalls song started to play,get money.This was a song all three of them vibed out to.Tyrelle set the Player onto the desk,then sat on the other side of John.

He placed bits of weed into a small white sheet,folding it up.He lit it afterwards,then passed it to John.Try it nigga,Joe whispered to John as the ashes fell to his towel.

John puffed,then exhaled.Tyrelle and Joe both laughed at John's facial expression.Give me a hit nigga,Tyrelle chuckled.John passed it to Tyrelle.Naw! Not like that,Tyrelle corrected.Inhale that shit,Tyrelle ordered.John puffed,inhaling the weed,and then passing it back over to Tyrelle again.

Nigga put your mouth over my lips dude,Tyrelle said in a whisper.Tyrelle placed his mouth next to John's,and then blew.John inhaled it,and then blew it out of his nose.

Lil dude,let me holla at you for a moment,Joe said,tilting his head to the left,wanting John to follow him.Tyrelle's face began to fume with anger as his nose flared.Im about to take a fucking nap John,wake me up,if i oversleep,Tyrelle said,stretching out on the bed.His muscular chest pointing to the ceiling.

John followed Joe to the other side of the room.Joe pulled the dividers back as John sat on the bed.Joe moved closer to John,his crotch almost pointing to John's face.

You gay right man? Joe asked in silence.I told you dude,i only tried something once,thats it,John answered.Did you like it? Joe questioned.It was alright,John replied.Dude wasn't your type or something? Joe said,waiting for John to reply.

Joe exposed himself through the slight slit in his towel,pulling his manhood to the edge of John's chin.John flinched.What chu doing dude? John whispered.I'll be gentle,Joe said,gently caressing John's face with one of his hands.He then pulled his hand towards John's waist,about to unwrap John's towel.

John heard feet stomping against the floor.A gun was now pointed at Joe's temple,it was Tyrelle.Tyrelle adjusted his towel,making sure it wouldn't fall from his waist,then squeezed John's arm.You was going let this nigga put his dick in your mouth dude! Tyrelle said,turning his gaze to John,his face swelling with anger,his eyes red and watery.

Joe placed his hands to the air,in a surrendering gesture.Nigga i know what this about,Joe chuckled.You want that lil nigga just as bad as i do,Joe smirked.

Shut the fuck up! Tyrelle yelled.This shit aint right,Tyrelle said,still squeezing John's arm.Why is this shit bothering you so much nigga? Joe chuckled.

Go ahead! Suck his dick John,watch me smoke both of ya'll motherfuckers! Tyrelle yelled with anger.Tyrelle began to breath heavily,this wasn't any type of anger,this was anger caused by envy.Calm down Tyrelle,John whispered,trying to get Tyrelle to come to his senses.

Aint no motherfucking calm down,you was going let this nigga fuck you too i bet,Tyrelle said,waiting for John to say something.

You wanna suck dick nigga! Okay,im going make you suck both our dicks nigga,and im going to let this nigga cum in your fucking mouth lil nigga.John saw Tyrelle mad before,but not this mad.

Get on your motherfucking knees nigga,Tyrelle commanded John.Tears fell from John's eyes,as he got to his knees.He could feel the water still dripping from Tyrelle's chest as Tyrelle towered over him.

A tear rolled down Tyrelle's face.You was the only one i ever trusted,and you pull this shit John! Tyrelle's deep voice echoed through the room.You was suppose to be my partner nigga! Tyrelle said,his voice exhausted.

Im still your boy! John yelled.I wasn't your partner when you was about to kill me awhile back,John explained.You really thought i could hurt you motherfucker? Tyrelle responded.

What's this then dude? John questioned.Tyrelle pulled John off his knees,showing John his arm.There was a slight scar on his arm,in the shape of the letter b.You remember this nigga? Tyrelle questioned.

Yea,i do,John replied,showing his arm as well.John had the same mark on his arm.Blood in and blood out motherfucker,for life,Tyrelle said,his eyes watering.

Tyrelle pulled john's arm towards Joe.You see that,this was my homeboy,we made a motherfucking pact,in blood.

He was all i had growing up,and you trying turn him into your fuck toy! Tyrelle yelled at Joe.Fuck this! Tyrelle said as he pushed John to the wall,restraining John's arms.His breath blew across John's bare chest.

Joe backed away,sitting in a chair,not sure what Tyrelle would do,if he moved.You know why this shit really fucked up John? Tyrelle said,pressing his body into John's.Because im feeling shit about you,shit that a dude not supposed to be feeling for another dude,Tyrelle said,his eyes watery and red.

Im going tell you straight up,nigga you had my shit so hard a few minutes ago,i wanted to kill your ass,for making me feel that fucking way,Tyrelle cried out.

Tyrelle kissed John on the lips,John didn't pull away,but let it happen.

The kiss was intense,passionate.Tyrelle wasn't the only one enjoying the kiss,John was too,but John could never fully express his feelings around Tyrelle,knowing Tyrelle was a ticking time bomb,waiting to explode.

Get the fuck out nigga,Tyrelle said,wanting Joe to exit the room.Joe left the room,heading back into his room with Lala.Lala slept through the commotion.

Tyrelle slid the door back,and then continued to kiss John.John was scared,but aroused also.Get on the bed nigga,Tyrelle whisperd in John's ear.

Chapter 7

Tyrelle turned off the lights,leaving only one on.John's nerves pushed to the surface.Take this shit off,Tyrelle said,ripping John's towel off,placing it under John's body.Tyrelle then tossed his towel from his waist,as he hovered over John.

We dont have any hats,John said silently.That's cool,we can take it slow the first time,Tyrelle whispered.

Tyrelle's manhood grew even more,once he and John's naked flesh touched.

Tyrelle pushed himself into John,grinding slowly.John turned his head to the side of the pillow,not wanting to look Tyrelle in the eyes.Naw,nigga turn your head back around,i want to see your facial expression,Tyrelle whispered quietly,his breath beating against John's neck.

John made eye contact with Tyrelle.Tyrelle began to push harder,after making eye contact with John,biting on his bottom lip as he forced himself into John.

Their bodies moved in a rhythm,sensual and passionate.Ah! John said,feeling himself about to climax.Tyrelle restrained John's hands,pushing his body into John's,this time he went faster,picking up speed.

Tyrelle moaned silently.Dude im about to cum,John said quietly,freeing his hands from Tyrelle's grip.John wrapped his arms around Tyrelle's back.Bust that shit,Tyrelle whispered,kissing the side of John's neck.

Tyrelle and John moaned in pleasure,as their bodies intertwined.Damn! Im about to nut,Tyrelle said in a strained voice,kissing John on the lips,as he erupted over John's chest,each drop of his essence spilling onto John's toned chest.

John reached a climax,just two seconds after Tyrelle.That shit felt good man,Tyrelle whispered,in a deep moan,resting his body on top of John's.

Yea,it was cool,John said,catching his breath.I never gave myself to another dude like that,John said quietly.Gave yourself? Nigga i took that shit,Tyrelle chuckled.And next time i want to be inside you,for real,Tyrelle said with a serious expression.

Yea whatever dude,John laughed.They both fell asleep,twenty minutes after their sexual encounter.

It was morning,the sun swept across John and Tyrelle's naked bodies.The only thing covering their loins was the thick blanket that covered the huge bed.

John opened his eyes,awakening to Tyrelle's gaze.Tyrelle was sitting in a chair,near the window,his naked body glistened in the sunlight as tiny drops of water dripped from his abs and face.

Nigga you slept like a motherfucking baby,Tyrelle chuckled as he dried off,placing on a pair of boxer briefs.

Go clean yourself up nigga,we about to roll out this camp.Alright,John said as he stood up,easing himself from the bed.Damn! I gotta pay my moms bill today,John said under his breath.At least i have enough money now,it can hold her bills down,for at least three months,John explained.

But damn,i still gotta worry about college.I missed a couple of classes already.

Nigga dont trip,i took care of your mothers bill already,Tyrelle said silently.That's why them motherfuckers haven't blown up my phone,John said.

Thank's man,John said,pushing his fist towards Tyrelle's.No problem dude,Tyrelle said with a calm expression.John headed towards the bathroom.Tyrelle grabbed John's arm,before John could make it halfway to the bathroom.

Let me holla at you for a minute,Tyrelle whispered.What we did last night was on some homey type shit,we boys,boys should be able to take care of each other,you feel me,but this stay between me and you man,alright,Tyrelle said silently.

For sure,John whispered.Cool then,Tyrelle said,placing on a white t and a pair of dark blue denim jeans.Tyrelle gave John's backside a quick glance as John headed into the bathroom.

Tyrelle shook his head,banishing the lustful thoughts from his mind,placing on his shoes in the process.John showered and then slipped into his clothes afterwards.Tyrelle stepped into Joe and Lala's room,waiting for John to gather his things.

Ya'll ready to hit the streets? Joe chuckled.Yea,we been ready,Tyrelle answered.What went down last night? I heard some things,Lala chuckled.

I dont know what the fuck this nigga told you,but keep this shit between us,you got me,Tyrelle said in a stern voice.

Naw! It ain't like that,i aint no snitch,but i wanna know what happened?Lala chuckled.Grown folks shit,Tyrelle answered.Did you fuck lil dude? Lala questioned silently.

Yea,he did,faggot ass nigga,Joe said with a angered expression.Faggot? This Nigga aint tell you that he tried to get my homeboy to suck his motherfucking dick,did he? Tyrelle said.

Oh shit! For real son,Lala chuckled.Nigga i be seeing the way you look at dude,Lala chuckled.Ay yo,keep this shit between us man,Joe whispered with a guilty expression.You brought the shit up nigga,Tyrelle said,while tucking his gun further down into his pockets.

Ya'll was trying gang bang the dude,Lala chuckled.John came out the slide door,noticing the room became quiet.Let's roll,Tyrelle said,nodding his head towards the door.

Two thumps hit the door.Who is it? Tyrelle answered in his deep voice.It's me,the bellboy.What you want? We about to head out anyway,Tyrelle said.John could hear other voices in the background.

It's somebody with him,John said in a low voice.What chu mean? Tyrelle questioned.Fuck this ethiopian motherfucker,kick that shit in,a voice said.The door flew open as two men with masks rushed through the door.The bellboy quickly fled the scene,knowing things were about to get worse.

Chapter 8

The men pushed their guns to Tyrelle and Joe,and Lala.John had pushed himself back through the slide door,before they could spot him.Ya'll motherfuckers work for Frank right? Ya'll motherfuckers shot up Rogers shit,and stole his motherfucking money,somebody about to answer in this bitch,The man explained.

Yea,we did motherfucker! Tyrelle shouted.Oh,so you think you tough motherfucker,one of the men chuckled,pushing his gun deeper into Tyrelle's skull.

There was a gagging sound as the man slightly lifted his mask,spitting in Tyrelle's face.

Fuck you nigga! Tyrelle yelled.Fuck all ya'll! Joe shouted.Im telling you,i would waist ya'll nigga's if i had the chance,Lala explained.

Bring that dike bitch over here,One of the men said calmly.John could hear everything taking place in the other room,his nerves were bolting through him.What the man said next,almost made John's heart stop.

Leave this bitch right here with me,and check the other room.Check the other room was the sentence that made John's heart nearly stop.John could hear Lala being smacked around,hearing the impact of the mans hand against Lala's face.He could also hear footsteps heading toward the slide door.

John panicked,unsure if he or Tyrelle or Lala or Joe would survive this.John's memories came rushing to him,in a flash.He pulled his pistol from his pants pocket.

At that moment,the man entered the door,spotting John on the floor.The mans eyes widened,seeing that John wasn't alone,but assisted by a black pistol,pointing in his direction.

There was gunfire.

Tyrelle jumped to his knees,his face angered and saddened.Im going kill all ya'll nigga's,this shit aint over son! Tyrelle yelled,his eyes puffy.

John!! John! Naw man! Dude aint answering,they killed my youngin! Tyrelle yelled in anger and agony.

Sit your ass back down nigga,that fool dead,the man chuckled.Tmane! What the fuck taking you so long? the man questioned,waiting for his side man to answer.

The man stepped to the edge of the slide door,peeping in,while still pointing his gun at Tyrelle and the others.A single bullet pierced through the side of the mans head,painting the bullet and the walls with blood.

The man fell to the floor,as if he were taking a nap,but this was a nap that would last forever.

John! Is that you dude? Tyrelle questioned as he headed to the slide door.Tyrelle entered the room,his eyes gazing upon John in relief.

John sat on the floor,panting back and forth,his heart racing.

It's alright man,we good,we good,Tyrelle said repeatedly,burying John in his pecks.This was the first time Tyrelle showed any emotion towards anyone.

John dropped the gun from his hand,slowly,letting the gun slip from his fingers.John had never taken lives before,but this was the first,and maybe not the last.

Tears rushed from John's eyes,but his tears weren't alone,being accompanied by Tyrelle's.

Joe and Lala stepped in,patting John on the head,they respected him.They all exited the room,stepping over the dead bodies that laid on the floor of the room.

Blood in and blood out,my dude,Tyrelle whispered continuously as he cradled John in his arms tightly,guiding John to the door as they all left the hotel.

This was only the beginning,the threat wasn't over,more blood would soon be spilled.Chaos would follow them to the next chapter,but for now they had peace.

The end.

Epilogue: Frank cleaned his house of the carnage left behind,after the assault.Frank had many connections,and some of the feds were apart of those connections.Frank loaded his gun,and so did his men.The shootout had become notorious in the streets,talked about by many.

Call Tyrelle and John,Joe and Lala should be with them.I need everyone on this job,we're taking the fucking streets back,Frank said with conviction,tapping the barrel of his gun on his bullet riddled table.

www.ingramcontent.com/pod-product-compliance
Lightning Source LLC
Chambersburg PA
CBHW031238280526
45784CB00004B/1623